CELEBRATE THE UNITED STATES!

WHY DOES THE FLAG HAVE STARS AND STRIPES?

BY BEATRICE HARRIS

Gareth Stevens PUBLISHING

Please visit our website, www.garethstevens.com. For a free color catalog of all our high-quality books, call toll free 1-800-542-2595 or fax 1-877-542-2596.

Cataloging-in-Publication Data
Names: Harris, Beatrice.
Title: Why does the flag have stars and stripes? / Beatrice Harris.
Description: Buffalo, NY : Gareth Stevens Publishing, 2026. | Series: Celebrate the United States! | Includes glossary and index.
Identifiers: ISBN 9781482470994 (pbk.) | ISBN 9781482471007 (library bound) | ISBN 9781482471014 (ebook)
Subjects: LCSH: Flags–United States–History–Juvenile literature. | Flags–Laws and legislation–United States–Juvenile literature. | Flags–United States–Etiquette–Juvenile literature.
Classification: LCC CR113.H3177 2026 | DDC 929.2′20973–dc2

Published in 2026 by
Gareth Stevens Publishing
2544 Clinton Street
Buffalo, NY 14224

Designer: Jeffrey Taylor
Editor: Therese Shea

Photo credits: Series art (blue background) Paladin12/Shutterstock.com; Cover, p. 1 Nana_studio/Shutterstock.com; p. 5 jonathandav/Shutterstock.com; p. 7 Rowanwindwhistler/commons.wikimedia.org; p. 9 Nana_studio/Shutterstock.com; p. 11 eugenesergeev/Shutterstock.com; p. 13 Wirestock Creators/Shutterstock.com; p. 15 Army Institute of Heraldry/commons.wikimedia.org; p. 17 Your Hand Please/Shutterstock.com; p. 19 AI Generated/Shutterstock.com; p. 21 (inset) Bumble Dee/Shutterstock.com; p. 21 Limolida Design Studio/Shutterstock.com.

Printed in the United States of America

CONTENTS

Boldface words appear in the glossary.

A Powerful Symbol

The U.S. flag is a **symbol** of the country. It represents, or stands for, the United States. The flag's **design** has changed over the years, but the stars and stripes have always been a part of it. They have special meaning. Read on to learn more about our national flag!

Stripes

The U.S. flag has always had 13 stripes. Seven stripes are red, and six stripes are white. The stripes are a reminder of the nation's beginnings. In 1776, 13 North American British **colonies** became the first 13 U.S. states.

New Hampshire
New York
Massachusetts
Rhode Island
Connecticut
Pennsylvania
New Jersey
Delaware
Maryland
Virginia
North Carolina
South
Carolina
Georgia

Stars

The flag has changed 27 times since 1777. As new states joined the country, new stars were added to the blue rectangle in the upper left corner. Since 1960, the U.S. flag has had 50 white stars to represent the 50 U.S. states. Each star has five points.

Colors

The colors of the flag—red, white, and blue—are the colors of the British flag. That may be why they were chosen for the U.S. flag at first. An early American leader named Charles Thomson said that red means bravery, white means goodness, and blue means **justice**.

A Short History

In the early days of the country, there were many American flag designs. The first official flag was **adopted** in 1777. It had 13 stars and 13 stripes, but people placed the stars in different ways on different flags.

The U.S. Flag Code

In 1942, U.S. Congress adopted a flag code. The code is a set of rules that says how the flag should look, including its measurements. It says how and when the flag will change if new states are adopted. It also says how people should treat the flag.

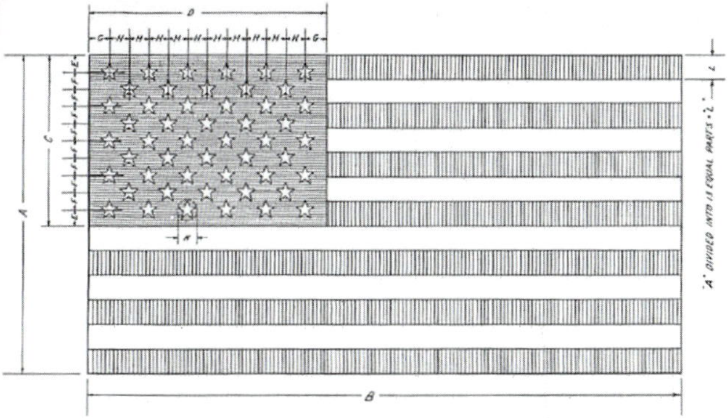

NOT TO SCALE

THIS IS A REDUCTION OF THE ORIGINAL

STANDARD PROPORTIONS									
HOIST (WIDTH) OF FLAG 1.	FLY (LENGTH) OF FLAG 1.9	HOIST (WIDTH) OF UNION .5385 (7/13)	FLY (LENGTH) OF UNION .76	.054	.054	.063	.063	DIAMETER OF STAR .0616	WIDTH OF STRIPE .0769 (1/13)
A	B	C =	D =	E =	F =	G =	H =	K =	L =

STANDARD SIZES															
	DIMENSIONS IN FEET AND INCHES										DECIMAL EQUIVALENT				
			DIMENSIONS OF UNION JACK THOSE USED BY ARMED FORCES												
NO OF LINE	A	B	C =	D =	E =	F =	G =	H =	K =	L =	A	B	C =	D =	K =
1	20'-0"	38'-0"	10'-9 1/4"	15'-2 3/8"	12 33/64"	12 33/64"	15 13/64"	15 13/64"	14 25/32"	18 15/32"	20.00'	38.00'	10.77'	15.20'	1.23'
2	8'-11 3/8"	17'-0"	4'-9 13/16"	6'-9 5/8"	5 25/32"	5 25/32"	6 49/64"	6 49/64"	6 19/32"	8 17/64"	8.95'	17.00'	4.82'	6.80'	.55'
3	5'-0"	9'-6"	2'-8 1/4"	3'-9 5/8"	3 7/32"	3 7/32"	3 51/64"	3 51/64"	3 22/32"	4 39/64"	5.00'	9.50'	2.69'	3.80'	.31'
4	3'-6"	6'-7 7/8"	22 5/8"	2'-7 15/16"	2 1/4"	2 1/4"	2 21/32"	2 21/32"	2 37/64"	3 15/64"	3.50'	6.65'	1.88'	2.66'	.22'
5	3'-0"	5'-8 3/8"	19 7/16"	2'-3 3/8"	1 15/16"	1 15/16"	2 9/32"	2 9/32"	2 7/32"	2 49/64"	3.00'	5.70'	1.62'	2.28'	.18'
6	2'-4 7/16"	4'-6"	15 21/64"	21 19/32"	1 17/32"	1 17/32"	1 51/64"	1 51/64"	1 3/4"	2 3/16"	2.37'	4.50'	1.28'	1.80'	.15'
7	15 27/32"	2'-6"	8 35/64"	12"	55/64"	55/64"	1"	1"	63/64"	1 7/32"	1.32'	2.50'	.71'	1.00'	.08'
8	10'-0"	19'-0"	5'-4 5/8"	7'-7 1/4"	6 31/64"	6 31/64"	7 35/64"	7 35/64"	7 3/8"	9 15/64"	10.00	19.00	5.38	7.40	.62

← NOT FOR USE BY DOD

SPECIAL SIZES (NOT 1 TO 19)															
NO OF LINE	DIMENSIONS IN FEET AND INCHES										DECIMAL EQUIVALENTS				
	A	B	C =	D =	E =	F =	G =	H =	K =	L =	A	B	C =	D =	K =
1	7'-0"	11'-0"	3'-9 1/4"	5'-3 3/4"	4 17/32"	4 17/32"	5 5/16"	5 5/16"	5 5/32"	6 15/32"	7.00'	11.00'	3.77'	5.31'	.43'
2	6'-8"	12'-0"	3'-7 1/16"	5'-0"	4 5/16"	4 5/16"	5"	5"	4 59/64"	6 5/32"	6.67'	12.00'	3.59'	5.00'	.41'
3	5'-1 13/16"	6'-6"	2'-9 1/4"	2'-11 3/4"	3 11/32"	3 11/32"	2 63/64"	2 63/64"	3 27/32"	4 3/4"	5.15'	6.50'	2.77'	2.98'	.32'
4	4'-4"	5'-6"	2'-3 15/16"	2'-6 5/8"	2 13/16"	2 13/16"	2 3/16"	2 3/16"	3 13/64"	4"	4.33'	5.50'	2.33'	2.56'	.27'
5	5'-0"	4'-0"	19 7/16"	22 1/8"	1 15/16"	1 15/16"	1 27/32"	1 27/32"	2 7/32"	2 49/64"	3.00'	4.00'	1.62'	1.84'	.18'
6	18"	2'-2"	9 11/32"	12"	31/32"	31/32"	1"	1"	1 7/64"	1 25/64"	1.50'	2.17'	.81'	1.00'	.09'
7	7"	11"	3 25/32"	5 5/16"	3/8"	3/8"	7/16"	7/16"	27/64"	17/32"	.58'	.92'	.31'	.44'	.04'

NATIONAL FLAG

NOTES:

1. STATUTORY AUTHORITY
   SECTION 1791, 1792 REVISED STATUTES
   AS AMENDED (4 U.S. CODE 1, 2)
   EXECUTIVE ORDER No. 10834, AUGUST 21, 1959
   (FR DOC 59-7095, FILED AUGUST 24, 1959)
2. FLAGS TO BE MANUFACTURED IN ACCORDANCE WITH APPLICABLE CURRENT MILITARY AND FEDERAL SPECIFICATIONS
3. FABRIC AND HEADING TO BE AS SPECIFIED IN CONTRACT
4. CABLE NUMBERS OF COLORS
   AS CITED IN THE NINTH EDITION STANDARD COLOR CARD OF AMERICA
   RED - - - - - -70180
   WHITE- - - - -70001
   BLUE - - - - -70075
   YELLOW - - - -65001 (FOR FRINGE WHEN APPLICABLE)
5. SEE IMPLEMENTATION SHEET FOR EACH SIZE USED BY DEPARTMENT OF DEFENSE

SUPERSEDES TIOH DRAWING NO. 5-1-17 DATED 21 AUG 1959

REVISIONS			
No.	DATE	CHECKED APPROVED	REVISION
1	25 Sept 62	CAR	
2	30 DEC 75	[illegible]	[illegible] FROM LINE NO. 8

DEPARTMENT OF DEFENSE
DEPARTMENT OF THE ARMY
THE INSTITUTE OF HERALDRY

FLAG, NATIONAL
UNITED STATES
OF AMERICA
50 STAR UNION JACK

SCALE | DATE 25 APRIL 1967

DRAWN [signature] | CHECKED [initials] | EXAMINED [initials]

APPROVED FOR THE INSTITUTE OF HERALDRY, U.S. ARMY, CAMERON STATION, ALEX, VA.

[signature]

DRAWING NO. 5-1-17

4

Flag Day

The U.S. flag has its own special day. June 14 is Flag Day, or National Flag Day. It celebrates the day the United States approved the first flag design in 1777. Americans should put up their U.S. flags on this day.

Respecting the Flag

People honor the flag to show **patriotism**. They hang it on poles in yards, parks, and schools. They say the Pledge of Allegiance to the flag. This is a promise to be **loyal** to the nation. They stand and face the flag at sports events for the **national anthem**.

Different Names, Same Flag

The U.S. flag has **nicknames**. Some call it the "Stars and Stripes," "Old Glory," or the "Star-**Spangled** Banner." Respect for the flag is important to many Americans because it shows respect for the United States itself.

More Flag Facts and Customs

- Fly the flag from sunrise to sunset. Flags can be flown at night if lighted.
- A **half-mast** flag can mean the nation is saddened by the death of an important person or group of people.
- On Memorial Day, fly the flag at half-mast until noon, then raise it to the top of the pole.
- The flag shouldn't be allowed to touch the ground.
- An upside-down flag means great danger.

GLOSSARY

adopt: To accept something or start to use it.

colony: A piece of land under the control of another country.

design: The pattern or shape of something.

half-mast: The position of a flag below the top of its pole, as a way to honor a person or people who have died.

justice: Fairness.

loyal: Faithful or supportive.

national anthem: A country's official song, played or sung during public events.

nickname: A name for someone or something based on an actual name or a feature.

patriotism: Love for one's country.

spangled: Having many decorations.

symbol: A picture, shape, or object that stands for something else.

FOR MORE INFORMATION

BOOKS

Carr, Aaron. *American Flag*. New York, NY: Lightbox Learning Inc., 2023.

Taylor, Charlotte. *The Truth About U.S. Symbols*. New York, NY: Enslow Publishing, 2023.

WEBSITES

The American Flag and Other National Symbols
www.usa.gov/flag
Read more about the flag and other U.S. symbols, including the bald eagle.

United States Flag Code
www.legion.org/advocacy/flag-advocacy/flag-code
Learn more about flag traditions in the official U.S. code.

Publisher's note to educators and parents: Our editors have carefully reviewed these websites to ensure that they are suitable for students. Many websites change frequently, however, and we cannot guarantee that a site's future contents will continue to meet our high standards of quality and educational value. Be advised that students should be closely supervised whenever they access the internet.

INDEX